# Wheels Around Inverness-shire

## Robert Grieves

Walter Alexander & Sons Ltd. of Falkirk, a member of the SMT group of companies, spread its wide portfolio of services after the Second World War with the acquisition of firms in the Inverness area although having already a base in the town at Longman Road, Needlefields, for their Inverness-Nairn-Elgin-Aberdeen corridor. First purchase was the town service network of William Greig in December 1947, along with sixteen mainly elderly double deckers and four even older single deckers. This takeover was followed in April 1948 when Alexander bought the infrequent Inverness to Balloch service via Culcabock and Smithton operated by James Mackintosh of Cantraywood, Croy. This was an unlikely purchase, especially since Mackintosh retained his original service commenced in 1922 between Croy, Culloden and Inverness until 1964 when he sold this remaining part of his business to Highland Omnibuses. Pictured in 1952 is "Jimmy Croy" as he was known, arriving in Strothers Lane, Inverness and passing the Macrae & Dick garage. Jimmy, wearing bunnet as usual, is at the wheel of ST 7657 his dark blue 14 seater Fordson which had been new in 1934 to Mackenzie Bros. of Port Henderson from where it had operated to Gairloch and in summer to Achnasheen. Jimmy Mackintosh had a lucky escape when this bus was damaged beyond repair caused by a tree toppling and crushing it during a storm, after which it was replaced by YS 2611 a former MacBrayne Bedford WTL. An unknown cyclist pedalling towards Academy Street neatly balances this glimpse of Inverness as it was.

ST 1349 is believed to have been the first motor fire tender in Inverness. It was a 20 h.p. model T Ford which arrived in 1919 with very basic bodywork built in the town by local coachbuilder Fraser of Fraser Street, especially when compared with today's sophisticated applicances fitted with an array of accessories. The fireman in the passenger seat is holding a puppy, perhaps for good luck. While researching for this book I came across an advertisement dated 1926 in which Inverness Town Council offered a Merryweather steam-powered fire engine for sale and invited offers. Also included were "four lengths of suction hose, a set of stoking irons and a box of tools". This machine was no doubt surplus to requirements after delivery of a new model.

## Acknowledgements.

Included amongst those who assisted with information and photographs I must thank the Biggar Albion Foundation, Alan Cross, George Heaney, late Jack Lumsden, Ian Maclean, Mary MacIntyre, G. Irvine Millar, The Omnibus Society, W. Gordon Steele, Neil Thexton, and John Sinclair.

# Introduction

Inverness-shire was Scotland's largest county, covering 4210 square miles and included the Hebridean islands of Skye, Harris, North Uist and South Uist. Local government reorganisation in 1975 saw the name disappear and the altered area became part of Highland region. Since Skye and Lochalsh was the subject of an earlier book in the "Wheels Around" series, as was Fort William and Lochaber, we now concentrate on the mainland part of the county, with emphasis on the eastern area around the Highland capital. The usual miscellany of nostalgic transport interest is included, featuring passenger vehicles in particular.

Summing up Inverness as it was half a century ago is this classic view of the now pedestrianised High Street in 1952, at its junction with Castle Street. Woolworths' store, only recently gone, has a Ford "Y" type of 1934 parked outside, with a pre-war Vauxhall driving past. Heading towards the camera is CST 636, a 1948 Austin 16 followed by DST 117 an Albion Clansman lorry of 1949 owned by local haulier John Robertson. Also visible are Austin, Ford and Morris cars plus no less than six bicycles.

Roderick Macrae, proprietor of the Lovat Arms Hotel in Beauly joined in a business partnership with William Dick of Redcastle in 1878. The new firm offered horses and horse-drawn carriages for hire and acted as a posting concern. Doctors were targeted in early advertising for the company: *Medical gentlemen will find this establishment a great convenience as Macrae & Dick propose keeping a comfortable brougham for night visitations and the ostler stays on the premises in Academy Street.* Their well-known four-in hand coach "May Queen" continued to ply with tourists from Station Square in Inverness to Culloden Battlefield until the outbreak of the First World War, by which time M & D also operated motor charabancs on tours from the town. With the arrival of the motor car around the turn of the century the horse side of the business declined. Cars increased in popularity and the company soon built upon the success of the automobile, opening large new garages at Inverness and Nairn. This Edwardian scene shows part of the workshop area in the Strothers Lane garage, where in the foreground we see an Alexandria-built Argyll, which was one of a fleet of taxis operated by Macrae & Dick in the Highland capital.

In contrast are these two large Humber hire cars, typical of Macrae & Dick's chauffeur-driven fleet in the 1950s. Seen outside the Strothers Lane premises are two examples dating from 1951, headed by Edinburgh registered JSF 357.

A 1913 advertisement for Macrae and Dick motoring services which illustrates one of their Arrol-Johnston hire cars.

Macrae and Dick were always quick to act on any new developments and registered one of the earliest motor buses in the county. This was in May 1910 when Halley charabanc ST 221 commenced to operate a selection of day and afternoon tours from Inverness. Licensing records reveal that this pioneering vehicle was smartly finished in a yellow livery with blue lining. It is seen at Temple Pier, Drumnadrochit, from where the tourist passengers returned to town by boat on Loch Ness. As may be noticed, the main road (now the A 82) to Fort William at that time had an unmetalled surface which could be a dustbowl in dry weather or a quagmire in the wet.

A speciality of Macrae and Dick, especially in Edwardian times, was the hire of cars and chauffeurs to transport prosperous families, mainly from England, during their Highland holiday. Also a small fleet of charabancs was maintained to cater for the developing tourist trade in the area. In June 1926 the company started their first regular bus services, running between Inverness and Fort William. initially in competition with MacIntyre of Fort William, but later sensibly operating in conjunction. Another service started at the same time ran to Nairn via Culloden and Croy, while the route to Tomatin and Garbole was a later development. The upper view shows GJ 2391, a second hand fourteen seater Chevrolet bodied by Thurgood of Ware, Herts., which M & D operated in the early 1930s on the Fort William service and is seen here at Fort Augustus. For some years 14 seaters were the maximum size of bus permitted on this route owing to restrictions placed on the fragile wooden bascule bridges across the Caledonian Canal.

*Left*: Farraline Park Bus Station, in 1952, after the Macrae & Dick's bus side of the business was absorbed into the newly-formed youngest member of the Scottish Bus Group, Highland Omnibuses Ltd., along with Walter Alexander's Inverness area services. All three buses are still in the livery of their former owners, blue and cream with Alexander and chocolate and cream with M & D, although carrying Highland fleet numbers. From the left are former Alexander R369 (AFG 679) of 1935, an Alexander bodied Leyland Titan TD4 and numbered J151 with Highland; CS 3895 a 1936 Albion Victor bodied by Stewart of Wishaw and new to A1 services of Ardrossan, prior to purchase by Macrae & Dick, later numbered AP108 by Highland ; XS 4409 was a six wheel Cowieson bodied Albion Valkyrie new in 1937 to Young of Paisley which passed to M & D in 1947 via Milne of Montrose and went on to serve Highland as their A110 until withdrawal in 1955 when it managed a further lease of life albeit as a lorry with contractor Young of Avoch.

The main rival to Macrae & Dick's successful Inverness based motoring business was A. W. Chapman & Co. whose premises in Eastgate are pictured in 1920. Chapman's proprietor from 1910 was Wilmot Hanbury Fowke, seen here among his staff in front centre (with bow tie) who was later chief engineer and manager with the Highland Transport Co. from its inception as Inverness & District Motor Services in 1925 until acquisition by Highland Omnibuses Ltd. in 1952. Chapman's garage was the main Ford agency and the cars are the ubiquitous model T Fords which enjoyed a hugely successful existence from 1908 through to 1926 during which time over 15 million were built. On the left is ST 1544, a left hand drive example of 1920 while the other is the more conventional right hand drive model with uniformed chauffeur in attendance. Intriguingly a notice in the window advertises the "Inverness & Perth" motor service operating on Sundays only in 1920, but of which nothing further is known.

Driving over Drumochter in 1903 *en route* from Inverness to Edinburgh. In the early days of motoring Scotland boasted several home-based car manufacturers. In particular the three As which were Albion, Argyll and Arrol-Johnston all achieved notable success. Here is a new Argyll four cylinder 16h.p. tonneau of 1903, built in Bridgeton prior to the move in 1905 to a palatial new factory at Alexandria. This car was owned by the pioneering motor dealer and engineer Rossleigh of Edinburgh and was driven by the company chauffeur Thomas Morrison. At that date the arduous journey between the Highland capital and Scotland's capital by road could only be classed as a challenge. A contemporary road guide book described the surface of this main route as *poor and overgrown with grass in some parts*, which now seems incredible when compared with today's A9 highway. The first major reconstruction and resurfacing work took place between 1925 and 1928, hampered by a general strike and bad weather. Motor registration numbers were not generally introduced until January 1904 explaining their absence on this car, although Inverness County Council started their "ST" series in December 1903.

ST 32, an Arrol-Johnston six seater solid tyred car of 1904 driving from Drumnadrochit to Dochgarroch on the main road of the time along the north side of Loch Ness which was then little more than a country lane. The owner was Colonel Lionel Dudley MacKinnon of Dochgarroch Lodge who has two young lady passengers, neither of whom is driving. Lest you should be curious the driving position on the Arrol-Johnston six seater was in the middle row with the rear row facing backwards. This antiquated style of car was in production from the late 1890s at the original Camlachie factory in Glasgow's east end and continued from 1901 to 1905 at the Paisley premises, achieving renown as being rugged and reliable, despite its outdated appearance. The four seat model was described by the company as a dog cart whereas the six seater was a car. Colonel MacKinnon kept ST 32 until 1908 when he sold it to Alex Bowman, a carriage hirer of Kirkintilloch who operated it as a taxi for several more years. In those early days of the motor car their cost was well out of reach of almost everyone apart from the wealthy few with Inverness-shire no exception. ST 1 and 2 were both steam cars: 1 was a French Gardner-Serpollet from Paris and 2 an American-built Toledo from Ohio registered respectively to Granville Hugh Baillie of Dochfour at his London town house and to James Leslie Fraser of Daviot Lodge. Other prominent names in the county with early cars were the Right Honourable Simon Fraser, Baron Lovat of Lovat, Beaufort Castle with Panhard ST9 and Alfred Donald, Mackintosh of Mackintosh, of Moy Hall. The Mackintosh owned several cars in those pioneering days including ST 60, a Wolseley, ST 64 a Daimler and ST 86 a Siddeley all in the space of a year between summer 1905 and 1906. The ST 1 number was famously used many years later on a Volvo P1800 driven by Roger Moore as private detective Simon Templar in the popular 1960s TV series "The Saint".

Feshie Bridge crosses a gorge over the river Feshie, a tributary of the Spey a little east of the village. This road, now the B970, provides a quiet alternative on the east side of the Spey to the busy main route between Kingussie and Grantown. ST 200 was an Overland landaulette, a product of the Willys-Overland Company of Toledo, Ohio. It was new in 1914 to Ewen Campbell & Son, garage proprietors of Main Street, Kingussie and replaced their original 1909 car with the same number at a time when re-registration was common practice. This local family firm enjoyed good trade by hiring cars and drivers to affluent visitors at the various local shooting lodges. The business later passed to Joseph McCormack of Kingussie.

Driving towards Newtonmore from Kingussie in 1919 is GA 4891 an Angus-Sanderson tourer which was new that year, the first for production of this make. Despite its Scottish sounding name, this car was built initially in Birtley, Co. Durham. The Angus-Sanderson was largely an assembled car incorporating a Tylor engine, Wrigley gear box, Woodhead suspension and Goodyear disc wheels. Although a good-looking product, this make never achieved enough sales to allow sufficient success for survival and despite a revival after a move to Hendon, manufacture ended in 1927.

The back of a bus can by no stretch of the imagination be described as beautiful, indeed personal insults often make derogatory facial comparisons between the two. However, transport enthusiasts find beauty where no one else can, as in these fleet names and varying styles of vehicles operated by Inverness-shire bus owners of the past.

*Below*: Alex MacIntyre and Sons of Fort William shared the service between Fort William and Inverness in conjunction with Macrae & Dick on a week about basis in the 1930s, and additionally held the Royal Mail contract. Appropriately the fleet livery was post office red. ST 6535 was one of several Ford 14 seaters used on this service and bodied by Jennings of Sandbach, Cheshire. In 1937 MacIntyre sold the business to David MacBrayne.

*Left*: Alex and John MacPherson of Gordon Square, Fort William served routes from the Fort to Corpach and Glenfinnan. ST 4068 of 1926 was a Chevrolet bodied by Alexander Motors of Edinburgh and finished in MacPherson's smart crimson colours. The company sold out to David MacBrayne in 1939.

*Above*: ST 6154 was a 20 seater Commer charabanc of 1930 with fully extending canvas hood and also built by Alexander Motors of Edinburgh. It was a member of Macrae and Dick's touring fleet which ran to a wide variety of beauty spots within range of Inverness.

*Top left*: Walter Alexander & Sons Ltd., whose HQ was in Falkirk, operated the original blue and cream "Bluebird" coaches on services to Inverness from Aberdeen, Elgin and Macduff and from Glasgow during the summer season. K68 (WG 7506) was an Alexander bodied Leyland Cheetah of 1938 with steps up the back to the rooftop luggage hopper, an important item in those days.

*Bottom left*: MacBraynes buses were a familiar sight in Inverness-shire from Mallaig in the west through to the Highland capital in the east. Seen here is no.106 (CGE 199), a Duple bodied Bedford WTB of 1939 picking up passengers on the bridge at Invermoriston en route for Fort William. This bus featured in the Scottish Motor Show that year and was sold in 1952 to MacKay of Tain.

*Top Right*: 58 (BST 918) of the Inverness based Highland Transport Co. was a Guy Arab of 1947 with bodywork also by Guy Motors and a popular choice with the company which was the major constituent of the newly formed Highland Omnibuses in 1952 where this bus continued to operate until 1962. The Highland Transport Co. eagle logo (centre) continued in use albeit in different form by Highland Omnibuses and later by Rapsons.

INVERNESS TO WHITEBRIDGE MAIL SERVICE
MOTOR LEAVING POST OFFICE.

The Stratherrick mailbus for Whitebridge about to leave Inverness Post Office in Queensgate prior to the First World War when the service was operated by Donald McGillivray of the General Store, Gorthleck. This was an Albion 16 h.p. model A4 and had been new in 1907 to Mackay of Achnasheen who sold it to McGillivray in August 1908, hence the Ross-shire number JS 86. Around 1912 Simon Fraser of Gorthleck became the regular driver of the mailbus and in 1916 he assumed ownership and continued to run the Stratherrick mail for 28 years until selling out to David MacBrayne in 1944 who continued to operate Fraser's two buses (Bedford ST 8681 and Dodge AST 616) for several more years. Other makes which had previously served with Simon included Chevrolet, DeDion, Fiat, Reo and Studebaker, mostly in Fraser's distinct yellow livery. Despite the change of ownership MacBrayne's Stratherrick mailbus was perhaps inevitably referred to as "Simon's bus" for many years after. Referring once more to the illustration above, the small man standing on the running board next to the huge load of parcels and mail secured by a tarpaulin, is Murdo Fraser of Fraser & Fland's garage, Inverness, where servicing and repairs were carried out on Simon's buses.

B.9. Tomich And Beauly Motor Service.

James Maclean of Beauly was quite an entrepreneur, owning a licensed grocery business and the Lovat Arms Hotel in the town plus the shop and post office at Tomich and later the Cannich Hotel . He was also owner of ST 412 an Albion 16 h.p. charabanc which entered service in June 1912 between Tomich, Cannich and Beauly, where it is seen at the railway station. Standing in the foreground is Robert Kennedy of Kiltarlity who was a regular driver at the time on Maclean's bus and who later operated his own bus service between Glenconvinth and Inverness. Noteworthy in this picture are the happy smiling faces of everyone aboard, despite the fact that passenger comfort was minimal and had not improved over the five years which had elapsed since the 1907 model of Albion seen on the previous page. The lady on board is certainly taking no chances that her big bonnet might be blown away en route as she has secured it with a stylish silk scarf. In comparison, observe the extremely subdued appearance of those on the Whitebridge bus. Perhaps they knew what lay ahead.

The colourful buses of David MacBrayne were well-known from one side of Inverness-shire to the other for over six decades and deserve a few pages of our attention. Their first bus service was operated in Inverness-shire and commenced in December 1906 between Fort William and North Ballachulish, a run which had been started in 1905 by the North British Railway Company, but was abandoned in June 1906. MacBrayne's first bus was a second hand Daimler which came all the way from the Isle of Wight, followed in 1907 by their first new bus, seen above at Onich Post Office. G 1091, registered in Glasgow, home of MacBraynes head office, was an Albion 16 h.p. "A3" model from their Scotstoun factory and its primitive bodywork, open to the elements, was built by David Stirrat & Son of Port Dundas, an old established Glasgow coachbuilder founded in the 18th century, but whose business closed prior to the First World War. A similar Albion (G 1327) arrived a few months later followed by a change of choice to Commer chassis. Although the MacBrayne fleet was finished in post office red livery from the earliest days, contemporary reports reveal that one of these first Albions was painted in "light chocolate".

David MacBrayne gradually established other services in the county including between Inverness and Glenurquhart and Inverness to Fort William in 1911. These runs were served by Commers bearing names rather than numbers such as Hare, Hound, Stag, Weasel and Wolf and with basic charabanc bodies whose only concession to comfort was a canvas hood and which had a large container for luggage, parcels and goods on the back. This illustration clearly shows these features and was taken in 1912 at the MacBraynes shed near Corriemony built to house the vehicle operating the Inverness-Drumnadrochit-Glenurquhart service. This wooden structure had a primitive bothy area to the rear which could house a driver sleeping there overnight, but hardly five star accommodation. During my own years as a driver with MacBrayne in the 1960s I recall the late Angus Ross of Inverness telling me of how he would sleep on weeknights in the Corriemony bothy (enduring the rigours of mid-winter in one of the coldest corners of Glenurquhart) and return home on Saturday nights on his bicycle. On one occasion his bus suffered a broken spring on Loch Ness side but he garaged it as usual then pedalled back to Inverness with the spring tied to his bike. There he collected a replacement which again he tied to the bike, returning to Corriemony where he had his bus fit again for service by Monday morning. Those were the distant days when drivers also maintained their vehicles which they invariably regarded as their own.

MacBrayne's Glenurquhart service was started in competition with the grandly named Glenurquhart Motor Car Co. Ltd, which had commenced operations in 1910 on what was at that time a busy rural run serving a then well-populated Glenurquhart and the village of Drumnadrochit before heading to the Highland capital via the shores of Loch Ness. Owners were Inverness based Munro and Gordon (Munro, a solictor and Gordon a draper/hatter) and as with MacBrayne's vehicle purchases for this route, Commer was the chassis of choice. ST 256 is seen when new in 1910 at Station Square Inverness (with driver Horsburgh) and was a 32 h.p. model from the Luton stable finished in a green livery lined in black. In 1911 when MacBrayne came on the route in opposition to the local company various tactics were used to combat the competition. MacBrayne attempted to gain custom by supplying tea and pies to prospective passengers at Inverness and also occasionally provided free travel proving that marketing methods have changed little over a century. Eventually the Glenurquhart firm admitted defeat and withdrew their service leaving David MacBrayne to continue until 1970 when Highland Omnibuses took over. Today the Glenurquhart service runs additionally through to serve Cannich and Tomich, although the original terminus at Corriemony no longer benefits from a bus.

Unlikely though it may seem today, three operators shared business on the rural route between Inverness and Glenurquhart until 1936 at a period when few folk owned a car and were accordingly much more dependent on bus travel. Apart from David MacBrayne who was longest established on the service, Charles MacDonald of Glenurquhart plied with a Chevrolet, as did John MacFarlane of Kilmartin. Complying with the decision of traffic commissioners all fares on the journey were common amongst the three owners, thus any attempted undercutting for extra business was not permitted. In 1936 MacDonald gave up his business, selling to rivals David MacBrayne (although not his bus). In 1945 MacFarlane did likewise and since his Bedford was still in good condition MacBrayne continued to operate it as their number 54 until 1952 when it was sold for further service to Gorman of Coatbridge. Illustrated is John MacFarlane taking delivery in 1937 of ST 9181, his new Bedford WTB with twenty seat bodywork built by Walker of Aberdeen which incorporated a compartment at the rear for goods and luggage and which replaced ST 5804 his fourteen seater Chev. of 1929. From 1945 onwards MacBrayne remained the only operator serving Glenurquhart and continued thus until acquired by Highland Omnibuses.

*Above*: Hazards encountered on MacBrayne's Foyers service in 1948 included this tight hairpin bend coming up from lower Foyers en route to Inverness via Glen Lia, Inverfarigaig and Torness on what was still partly an unsealed road. With a wide swing in a bus with a reasonable steering lock it was just possible to get round in one attempt, as seen with Duple bodied Bedford WTB no.58 (BGE 627), new in 1938.

*Top right*: Tight squeezes were often experienced when passing the many timber wagons in the area when trees were felled in 1948. Making for Foyers, no. 58 edges past a laden lorry by means of mounting the grass verge. This bus was withdrawn by MacBrayne in 1952 when it was purchased for further passenger service by McCormack of Kingussie who operated to Grantown on Spey.

*Lower right*: These three photos were taken on the same day when Bedford no.58 had a further encounter with a timber lorry. CSA 951 was a Leyland Beaver new in 1946 to Sutherland of Peterhead but by 1948 operated by haulier John Nicol whose driver is seen guiding the Foyers-bound bus past the Beaver with a couple of inches to spare while his mate watches from above.

Representative of the mixture of vehicles operating in the MacBrayne fleet during the 1950s is this scene at Farraline Park showing three of the buses based at Inverness but which would usually stay overnight at their outer terminal point often adjacent to the driver's house. On the left is 152 (KGB 263) on the Whitebridge service, one of 22 Bedford OLAZ chassis delivered in 1952 with Duple bodies which varied in seating capacity from 14 to 25 dependent on the size of the luggage/mail compartment at the rear which many incorporated. Some of the Commers also had these compartments which reduced their normal 29 seat capacity and Croft bodied no. 99 (FUS 679) is seen prior to departure on its regular run through the Great Glen to Fort William. No.64 (EGA 641) was an A.E.C. Regal with 35 seat Park Royal coachwork, one of nine delivered in 1947 and crew-operated on the Glenurquhart service.

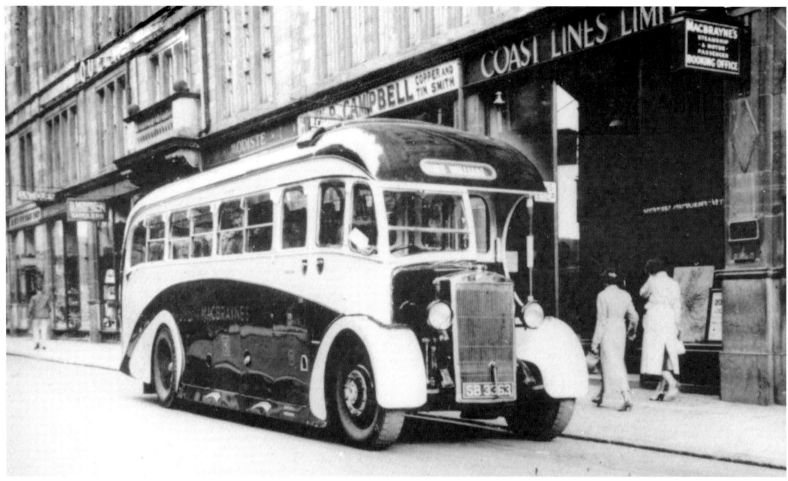

Queensgate in Inverness, which today is a one way street with traffic flow in the opposite direction, was at the time of this view in 1937 the terminus of MacBrayne's bus service to Fort William recently acquired from MacIntyre of Fort William. No.30 (SB 3363) is a Maudslay Meteor at the stance outside the office of associated company Coast Lines Ltd and which later became MacBrayne's Inverness office. This was one of four similar vehicles which had joined the fleet in 1929. Their petrol engines were replaced by diesels in 1936 when the original Hall Lewis coachwork was rebodied by Park Royal, incorporating rather ungainly long mudguards. Interestingly these rebuilt vehicles were the first to carry a variation of the red, green and cream livery which became so familiar with the company.

Regular day tours which operated during the summer season from MacBrayne's Fort William depot provided valuable extra revenue. One of the busiest was the Loch Ness circular tour which covered both sides of the famous loch from Fort Augustus, but without any guarantee of seeing you know who. A popular pause was made at Urquhart Castle where 181 (605 CYS) is seen awaiting its passengers. This was a 29 seat Duple bodied Bedford C5 delivered in 1961 which later served with Highland Omnibuses as their no. C28.

Until the 1970s Station Square was the transport hub of Fort William where bus, boat and train all connected. Opposite the train station where we see a British Railways class 5 locomotive, MacBraynes had their bus station while their vessels would sail to and from the pier in the background on cruises to Oban and Iona. This bustling scene from 1959 shows Glenfinnan-bound MacBrayne no.23 (WGG 624) a Bedford C5 model with Duple (Midland) bodywork which was new that year and which in 1970 passed to Highland Omnibuses as their no.C3.

Snowy Strathnairn during the winter of 1956 -1957 with MacBraynes No.152 (KGB 263), a Duple bodied Bedford OLAZ new in 1952 which was the usual performer on the service between Inverness and Whitebridge. This style of vehicle was the last of the rather old-fashioned type of normal control or bonneted bus and epitomised MacBrayne's fleet on rural services for fifteen years or more, as they were a familiar sight on routes throughout the company territory on the mainland and the islands. The regular driver for many years of this Stratherrick mail bus was Tom Davis of Whitebridge, who had a key to empty the post boxes along the route via Gorthleck, Errogie, Torness, Aberarder, Flichity and Farr. The location is the bridge over the River Nairn at Balnafoich, heading for Inverness. Since 1916 the Whitebridge bus had been operated by Simon Fraser of Gorthleck who sold the business to David MacBrayne in 1944 along with one Bedford and one Dodge.

Whenever possible MacBrayne's bus services would link with steamers and ferries providing valuable transport connections. Awaiting arrival at Nether Lochaber for custom off the ferry from Ardgour in the late 1950s is no.19 (GUS 407) part of a large fleet of Park Royal bodied Maudslays new to MacBrayne in the late 1940s. This was one of several sold on withdrawal from service in 1963 to contractor Duncan Logan of Muir of Ord. It had diverted briefly from its journey between Kinlochleven and Fort William to reverse down the jetty to meet passengers and mail. On the opposite shore, visible across the Corran Narrows, MacBraynes ran a bus from Ardgour to Acharacle which connected with the service between Salen and Kilchoan at the western end of the Ardnamurchan peninsula.

A strange hybrid was this 2-ton road-railer vehicle which could be driven normally on the road network but was also easily adaptable to the railway system, dependent on circumstances. Registered AYH 947 in 1934 to legalise its road use, this dual purpose vehicle on a Huddersfield built Karrier chassis was used mainly for permanent way maintenance work and owned by the London & North Eastern Railway Company. Its road wheels were raised and lowered by crank action and transference from rail to road was effected by lowering them fully and running on to a rail-level ramp, so lifting the rail wheels clear of the metals. The versatile vehicle usually worked northwards from Crianlarich, using the road from there to Bridge of Orchy, a stretch with generally convenient access to the line, thence railway to Tulloch and back to the road from there to Fort William. On the Mallaig extension of the West Highland Railway it was run as a rail vehicle only, achieving savings for the LNER by the elimination of ballast engine workings and thus relieving rail traffic congestion. It is pictured eastbound on this line in 1936 at the platform of Glenfinnan Station.

Laggan Bridge carries the main Fort William to Inverness road across the Caledonian Canal on the section connecting Loch Lochy with Loch Oich. This was the scene in April 1921 looking towards the Laggan lock-keeper's cottage as the unaccustomed extra weight of a steam roller was causing some concern. Precautions had been taken to build up the bridge with reinforcing planks above the normal level of the roadway by about three feet and as the extra load steamed slowly over the artificial platform towards the Well of the Seven Heads, the procedure was watched anxiously by the waterways men. The engine, which was probably working on road repairs in the area, was an Aveling & Porter built in Rochester, Kent, whose prancing horse motif can just be discerned ahead of the chimney. At the time of this view, Laggan Bridge was of the double cantilever design, replaced in 1932 during the Great Glen road improvements by the swing bridge which stands today.

As motor traffic continued to increase, so also did pressure on the authorities to improve roads throughout the Scottish Highlands. Not least was the important link from Glasgow to Inverness via the western route and Fort William which had fallen into a deplorable condition. Following upon General Wade's original plans, little or nothing had been done to upgrade it to modern requirements and the northern section by Loch Ness side constructed by Thomas Telford in the early 19th century was still narrow and badly graded, with the surface especially bad along the shores of Lochs Oich and Ness. The first section from Glasgow to Loch Lomondside received attention in the mid 1920s but it was not until 1930 that work began on the 87 mile Highland section between North Ballachulish and Inverness. This was not fully completed until autumn 1937, despite the road having been officially opened in 1934. The huge construction task had been Scotland's biggest road rebuilding scheme since Telford's time and involved the removal of innumerable blind corners and replacing no less than 55 stone bridges and three canal bridges over this section alone. These scenes illustrate some of the difficulties encountered during the several years of upheaval along the Loch Ness side portion of the route, when motorists had to traverse most sections during the actual excavations with consequent damage to their vehicles. The huge nature of the task involved the laying of a temporary rail line on which a steam engine and wagons could transport road building equipment and materials for the project. This of course meant lengthy delays to traffic and especially to the long-suffering bus and lorry drivers who necessarily encountered these problems on a daily basis. Just visible in the above view from 1933 is the roof of a bus patiently waiting to pass the huge "steam navvy" and then cross the rail track past the locomotive. Winter conditions caused the euphemistically described "road" to degenerate into a morass of mud.

Again showing some of the abominable rock strewn surface of what passed as a road during the reconstruction of the A82. Motorists had little alternative but to grit their teeth and contend with a situation which stretched seemingly interminably section by section over a period of seven years. Halfway up the hill may be seen a petrol powered Simplex motorail wagon carrying construction materials for heavy grading work on this stretch of realignment east of Fort Augustus in 1933. Tenders were submitted by a large number of bidders for the work and the successful firms were based not only in Scotland but England and even Wales. The total distance was divided into seven sections from North Ballachulish to Inverness. For example section 5 from Invermoriston to Achnahannet (eight miles) was awarded to William Tawse of Torry, Aberdeen, who was situated nearer the work than any other of the contractors.

Those who suffered most during the upheaval of the roadworks included the passengers on the scheduled bus service between Fort William and Inverness, provided jointly at this period by MacIntyre of Fort William and Macrae & Dick of Inverness. Buses were often considerably delayed, but at least the local folk were forgiving for slow progress as they understood the reasons. Again these two scenes encapsulate just how bad the conditions could be, making a journey along the north side of Loch Ness more of a slalom through an obstacle course. The bus in both views is ST 6537, new in 1931, one of several Ford 14 seaters operated by MacIntyre of Fort William in post office red colours on the mail contract to Inverness. The destination board above the windscreen reads "Pioneer through bus Inverness & Fort William", referring to MacIntyre's fleet name. Broken springs and punctures, plus general damage to paint and bodywork were commonplace to both operators who must have breathed a great sigh of relief once the roadwork was complete. In the scene on the left the Ford squeezes between a pile of rock dislodged by the "steam navvy" and the loch side wall, while the upper view shows it inching past human navvies with their pneumatic drills on one side and a sheer drop into Loch Ness on the other.

### The Frigate Bird
#### Dom Romuald Alexander O.S.B.

The MacIntyre Bus is a beautiful thing;
Like a great frigate bird, it is swift on the wing.
It has linked up the Forts and for-aye either sea,
in the closest of bonds and a real unity.
Fort William at 9; Fort Augustus 11,
and if sometimes we fear it will land us in heaven,
how vain is that fear! there'll be no requiem,
for its driver - Young Macintyre's - simply a gem,
and we safely arrive Inverness 1 p.m.
The pace that it travels annihilates midges:
but why, gentle sirs don't you strengthen the bridges?

From 'The Great Venture' or Fort Augustus in Verse,
a book of poems by monks at Fort Augustus Abbey.

Prior to all the problems caused by the seven year renovation of the Fort William to Inverness main road the main difficulties encountered by motorists had been the hazards of blind bends and poor alignment of the narrow highway. Public transport operators were confined to the operation of 14 seaters because of restrictions on the various bridges across the Caledonian Canal. Seen here outside Stewart's General Stores at Drumnadrochit (now "Bits & Pieces") is one of a fleet of Fords owned by MacIntyre of Fort William, providing the cross country link between the Fort and the Highland capital. Archie MacIntyre has his arm across the front bumpers of ST 5347, a 1928 purchase, performing what was then a necessary action each time the engine required life. This was the often back breaking and sometimes literally wrist breaking task of cranking the motor with the starting handle, something which became a redundant exercise once self-starters were fitted. The attached poem, The Frigate Bird was penned in the late 1920s by one of the Benedictine monks at Fort Augustus abbey in praise of MacIntyre's bus service which was often used by the brothers.

By the time of this photograph in 1936 the A82 road along Loch Ness side had been completely reconstructed apart from the final 4.5 mile stretch from Inverness to Dochfour. The Great Glen road was officially opened in September 1934 by Leslie Hore-Belisha, the serving Minister of Transport who had been responsible for the introduction of pedestrian crossings and driving tests to Britain during the 1930s. Also present were notably the Mackintosh of Mackintosh, Sir Donald Cameron of Lochiel, Baroness Burton and Charley Tinker, Laird of Kilmartin (a retired Yorkshire industrialist and later Inverness County Council roads convener). The opening ceremony was held near Abriachan Pier and the road was named the Glen Albyn Highway. A contemporary motoring magazine then transferred the doubtful title of "worst road in Britain" from the A82 to the A830 between Fort William and Mallaig. This view at the Half Way House Alltsigh between Invermoriston and Drumnadrochit shows the much improved new road which allowed road haulage and passenger transport operators to reduce vehicle running times between Glasgow, Fort William and Inverness. The Half Way House (which today is the Loch Ness Youth Hostel) provided accommodation, meals and Esso petrol to passing motorists and had at least one customer on this occasion, visiting in WS 9181, an Edinburgh registered Austin 10 new in 1936.

Another of the many privately owned firms acquired by Highland Omnibuses was Robert Angus Robertson of Tomich, Strathglass, who sold his Tomich to Beauly service in 1967. For a brief period this had been extremely busy when the construction of the Mullardoch-Fasnakyle-Affric hydro-electric project between 1947 and 1950 caused a population explosion in the area. The influx of around 2,000 men staying in workers camps at Cozac and Cannich brought Robertson booming business which required several additional buses to cope, some purchased new. Pictured at Cannich before the boom is ST 8578, an Albion bought new in 1936 with 14 seat bodywork by Stewart of Wishaw incorporating a rear compartment for luggage and parcels. Unusually this type was based on a commercial or lorry chassis rather than a passenger model. This was the regular bus on the Strathglass service right through the wartime years. It was painted in dark brown livery and divided from the yellow upper works by a white waistband.

Gollanfield crossroads on the main Inverness to Nairn road was sadly the scene of a fatal accident in November 1938. A schoolgirl walking down from her home in Croy to the main highway to catch Alexander's bus to Nairn reached the crossroads as two buses arrived for Inverness. The first stoppped to uplift passengers and the girl crossed the road in front unaware that the second bus was overtaking. Despite the efforts of its driver she was killed and the bus toppled into the adjoining field. Walter Alexander & Sons had operated services on this section of road and onwards to Aberdeen since 1930 with their acquisition of the Scottish General (Northern) Omnibus Co. and also ran between Inverness and Nairn via Ardersier and Fort George. The ill-fated bus was one of their many "F" class Albion Valkyries of the early 1930s with Alexander's own bodywork, which was soon back in service after minor repairs.

The first regular bus service linking the Highland capital with Glasgow was provided by Highland Motorways of Glasgow, an independent firm which launched the first trip in May 1928. Sensibly this was shortly after the previously mediocre Great North Road through the Drumochter Pass had been upgraded, allowing a speedier journey. Even so this was still a day's travel with departure time from Glasgow at 9.15am and arrival in Inverness at 6.15pm. The vehicle used on the run was GE 1348 the 26 seater Talbot pictured above at Carrbridge Hotel in the dramatic black livery adopted by owner James Mackay MacGregor and broken by a contrasting waistband in MacGregor tartan. Passenger comfort was all-important and the interior of the coach (believed to have been bodied by Kelly of Parkhead, Glasgow) included curtained windows, fitted tables and luxurious seating, all unusual features for the period. The initial three days a week service was increased to daily in July 1928 but only ran during this first season. Alexander of Falkirk introduced a similar service between Glasgow and Inverness in 1929 which continued throughout their existence and even included an overnight journey during the summer for several years. The alternative bus route between Inverness and Edinburgh was pioneered in 1929 by Scott's Azure Blue Coaches of Edinburgh who boasted of their "luxury Daimler saloons", selling out in 1932 to SMT of Edinburgh who continued to maintain the inter capital service.

At the age of twelve in 1918 William Greig started work as a conductor with Roderick MacLennan, proprietor of a bus service between Inverness and Kessock Ferry. In 1927 Willie was able to purchase the firm and two years later also bought the bus side of the Kessock Ferry Company which had operated its own vehicles in conjunction with the ferries. Other local town services were started to Balliifeary, Culcabock, Dunain Road, Holm Mills and Leachkin and in 1933 Fraser and Eland's service to Culduthel was acquired and improved. Greig's assorted fleet over the years included Albion, Chevrolet, Crossley, Ford, Gilford, Guy, Leyland and Tilling Stevens makes and when the company sold to Alexander of Falkirk in 1947 the buses were mainly double deckers with sixteen passing to the new owner along with four single deckers. Illustrated is one of several former Sheffield Corporation Leyland Titans which were later incorporated with Alexander's fleet. This was WE 8780 of 1930 vintage seen outside Greig's Telford Street Garage during wartime when the white-tipped mudguards and masked headlamps were compulsory. It had been purchased directly after withdrawal from Sheffield in 1940 and was loaned by Greig to help wartime vehicle shortages in London during the winter of 1940/1, later receiving Alexander fleet no. R564 although only operating as such for a few months, being scrapped in 1948.

Another wartime scene which shows Greig's Telford Street garage opposite the former Inverness Caley football park, with former Central SMT Albion Valkyries, none of which passed to Alexanders. VD 1743 1733 and 1735 all had bodywork by Pickering of Wishaw and dated from 1932, with VD 1743 operating for Cruickshank & Ross of Newburgh, Aberdeenshire before acquisition by Greig. Colours of the Greig fleet varied over the years as from 1927 the original livery was blue with red waist band and white roof, changing during the 1930s to chocolate and cream (Greig's crews wore brown uniforms) and later to red and cream in which these Albions were painted. The garage extended at the rear through to Carse Road and on sale of the buses in 1947 Greig retained the frontage as a coachbuilding department while Alexanders took over the Carse Road end of the building as their garage, which passed to Highland Omnibuses on their acquisition of the town services in 1952. Alexander also had a depot on railway ground in Longman Road, Needlefields where their buses on the Nairn/Elgin/Aberdeen services were housed. Inset is an advertisement for Greig's from the mid 1930s.

A glimpse into the garage in the mid 1950s. This was the interior of Highland Omnibuses' Carse Road depot in Inverness at a period when several traditional Albions still featured in the fleet. Which contained a wide variety of vehicle types. Prominent is Valkyrie A111 (CST 649) of 1948 which was a Brockhouse bodied example inherited with the MacRae & Dick fleet in 1952, as was A106 (WG 4922). This was also a Valkyrie but with bodywork by Walker of Aberdeen which was new to Alexander of Falkirk in 1936, although had been ordered by Grey Line of Elgin who sold out to Alexander in 1935 prior to delivery of this bus. Also seen are two Guy Arabs, double decker E66 (CST 273) a Northern Counties bodied example new in 1948 to Highland Transport and single decker K80 (JWS 127) which was one of the first batch of former London Transport Guy double deckers rebuilt and rebodied by Scottish Omnibuses in 1952. The Carse Road premises had originally been the depot for William Greig's local services whereas the other Highland Omnibuses base was the former Highland Transport garage in Longman Road Needlefields next to Alexander's depot. The inadequate Carse Road garage was vacated when the spacious new depot and workshops opened at Seafield Road in 1972.

Decorated Academy Street at MacIver's store during Coronation year in 1953. This was the stance for services to the north prior to the opening of the bus station in 1957. About to depart for Hughton, the Kiltarlity bus was H98 (VD 4445), the unusual all-Leyland Tiger TS7T 6-wheeler inherited from the Highland Transport Company in 1952 and new in 1935 to Central SMT. Behind it is a Guy Arab 'decker, destination Dornoch, plus one of the former Alexander Leyland Titans on a town service. The Kiltarlity route was inherited by Highland Transport in 1937 with their acquisition of Fraser Bros of Allarburn.

Although the town bus station had been located at Farraline Park in the former Bell's school playground since the 1940s it was not until 1957 that a more formal area was laid out with proper stances for the various services which used the facilities. Incredibly, however, when the bus station was new little extra provision was made for the passengers as this scene verifies, with no shelters at the stances, although this was admittedly later remedied. On a damp day in the new bus station is Highland Omnibuses Leyland TD4 no. J157 (WG 3511) which was new in 1936 as single decker Leyland Tiger TS7 P327 in the Walter Alexander fleet before conversion in 1943 and transferring to Highland in 1952.

A typical town scene in the late 1950s shortly before these elderly Leyland 'deckers were withdrawn after providing the backbone of local services for over a decade in the Highland capital with Alexander then Highland Omnibuses. Bearing in mind that their chassis dated originally from the mid 1930s, these rebuilds from single deckers had a life span approaching 25 years, not insignificant for a hard worked public service vehicle. Leaving the stop in Academy Street at the Station Hotel is J153 (WG 3486) heading for Raigmore Hospital via Culcabock, while stationary is J154 (SN 7136) which had started life with David Lawson of Kirkintilloch; it is bound for Laurel Avenue via Ballifeary. PUS 702 is a Ford Thames "Luton" type van of 1956 on furniture deliveries and owned by the Scottish Co-operative Wholesale Society. Completing the scene is a series 1 Land Rover from the early 1950s.

A scene from 1957 in Farraline Park Bus Station where the clock shows 2.55, giving five minutes before departure of Highland's Guy Arab K98 on the long-established journey to Dornoch at 3pm. Registered LSC 99 this was one of eighteen similar vehicles reconstructed between 1952 and 1954 which worked with Highland Omnibuses and gave sterling service until the mid 1960s. All had been former London Transport double deckers delivered during wartime and purchased after withdrawal by Scottish Omnibuses of Edinburgh who built new 30 foot long bodies on the renovated chassis, all of which work was completed at their Marine Works in Portobello. Instead of the usual "Guy" badge on the radiator these rebuilds sported a badge with the name "Highland". On Saturdays this 3pm journey north was extended as far as Brora arriving there at 7.45pm but of course at that period there were no bridges over the firths thus explaining the lengthy running time.

In 1972 Highland Omnibuses introduced twelve Willowbrook bodied Ford R192 buses to the fleet, followed for the next five years by an annual intake of Fords. T73 (UST 873L), an R 1014 type which was one of the 1973 deliveries is seen crossing Ness Bridge with the castle dominating above. Some of this Willowbrook bodied batch including T73 were initially painted in Highland's blue and grey coach livery although later received the crimson lake bus colours. The destination Stornoway is misleading since this bus never operated in the Outer Isles where Highland had a base in Tarbert Harris, during the period 1970-1975 after acquiring the business of John Morrison of Northton and later David MacBrayne's Harris operations.

The original suspension bridge for road traffic across the Ness dated from 1855 and is pictured on the front cover. In 1939 a decision was made to replace the congested old bridge and accordingly a temporary wooden structure was built to ease the traffic load, which crossed the river to join Ness Walk at the Columba Hotel. Because of wartime problems followed by further hiccups the temporary bridge continued in existence for many more years than intended, sharing the traffic load along with the original until 1961 when today's Ness Bridge opened. During the period of demolition of the 1855 bridge the substitute structure carried all the town centre cross-river traffic for a period. Seen here is a third bridge which was constructed immediately upstream from the new crossing mainly as a working platform for contractors' vehicles, predominantly used by William Logan, carrying out demolition and building work between 1959 and 1961. Prominent on the temporary trestle structure is a Foden 22-RB lorry carrying a Ruston Bucyrus crane, while the rowing boat below was also involved in the proceedings.

The ferry Eilean Dubh was named in Gaelic after the Black Isle peninsula which is seen across the firth. Introduced as the first vehicle ferry on the crossing in the late 1940s she carried a maximum of eight cars. This view from South Kessock in the early 1960s shows her discharging her tightly packed cargo of cars with a Rover being guided ashore to be followed by Hillmans, a Standard and a Morris.

*Right*: An important transport link was the passenger connection from Inverness town centre to the ferry from the days of the horse-drawn coach, progressing through early solid tyred charabancs with the coming of the motor age and finally a frequent service of double decked buses. There had even been a proposal in 1903 to provide a tramway service to the ferry, although this was never adopted. Here we see the "ferry bus" as it was always known, on this occasion Leyland Fleetline/ECW no. D13 (SAS 855T), arriving at South Kessock terminal in 1980 when construction of the new bridge was progressing in the background. Foot passengers from the ferry await the bus which will shortly return to town. Highland Omnibuses and successors Highland Scottish provided the ferry link for 30 years from 1952 until it ceased to sail in 1982.

*Left*: Looking across the firth towards North Kessock showing the close connection between bus and ferry. D13 will soon depart via the town centre to Morvich Way. The final ferry, seen here, was the *Rosehaugh*, which on opening of the bridge in 1982, enjoyed a reprieve for a further few years on the west coast, on the sailing operated by Highland Council between Corran and Ardgour.

*Left*: For many years the name Robertson was synonymous with road transport around Inverness where different members of the family operated their own businesses. John Robertson developed timber and general haulage work, operating a fleet of dark blue Albions from his base in Shore Street; brother Charles specialised mainly in the movement of cattle and livestock from premises in George Street with lorries in contrasting blue colours, while Daniel Robertson & Sons adopted a green livery with red mudguards and was also mainly involved in carrying livestock. His garage was formerly in George Street and later in Longman Road at Seafield Road on the site later used as a bus garage and headquarters by Highland Omnibuses. Back in 1924, ST 2778 was a new Renault lorry supplied to Charles William Robertson of Queensgate, Inverness.

*Right*: Jumping 35 years, NST904 was an AEC "Mercury" of 1959 which worked in Charles W Robertson's fleet. On this occasion it has cattle float bodywork attached although C W Robertson also subcontracted his fleet to others for a variety of purposes. For instance a contract was held with Calder's Alloa Ales which if required could transform this lorry from carrying bullocks one day to beer the next.

*Right*: Some of John Robertson's mainly Albion fleet were contracted to other companies and painted in their colours. For instance, HST 788 of 1955 was a "Claymore" model with Homalloy cab and bodywork which operated in the green livery associated with Castrol motor oils. Seen when new in Ness Walk, looking across the river to the castle, it has a more modern look than its slightly younger stable mate of the same vintage seen below. This was due mainly to the cab styling and the lack of an exposed radiator, a feature which tended to give Albions an old-fashioned appearance before their time.

*Left*: Seen at Inverness Harbour, JST 555 was a six wheel Albion "Chieftain" supplied in 1955 by the Inverness Motor Co. (a Macrae & Dick subsidiary) to John Robertson of Shore Street. The bodywork was built and painted in Robertson's dark and light blue livery by J & J Ingram of Aberdeen.

Burnetts' bread was a household name in the Highlands for many years until dropped by the national bakery company which inevitably took over. Almost as familiar was the fleet of mid-green delivery vans based at Burnett's Needlefields bakery, including JST 258, an Albion "Claymore" of 1955 bodied by Gibson of Leith. Close inspection reveals the reflection of an Austin car on the gleaming paintwork of the cab door. This underfloor engined 4-tonner featured for a period in a contemporary advert for Albion Motors praising the "Claymore" model and cleverly titled "Bred" for the job.

A further purchase in the Inverness area was made by Alexander in June 1950 when Wemyss Bros of Ardersier sold out. Along with Wemyss' long-established service from Inverness to Ardersier and Fort George, Alexander acquired four assorted single deckers of AEC, Bedford and Dennis manufacture along with three modern Guy, Leyland and Crossley double deckers. Pictured is Leyland PD1A CST 256 of 1948, bodied to Leyland's attractive standard design by the Lancashire based Samlesbury Engineering Co. which received Alexander fleet no. RA105. On formation of Highland Omnibuses this Leyland was transferred to the new company where it was numbered J169 and remained until withdrawal in 1963.

Wemyss Bros. final purchase before acquisition by Alexander in 1950 was uncommon in the Scottish Highlands. It was a Crossley DD42/5 bodied by Roe of Leeds, delivered in September 1948 and registered CST 671, becoming Alexander's RO695. Unlike Wemyss' Leyland this Crossley did not pass to Highland Omnibuses and remained in the Alexander fleet until relatively early withdrawal in 1956 when it was sold for further service to Baxter of Airdrie. This was not the end, however, since it then passed to Todd of Whitchurch in 1960 and finally to Red Rover of Aylesbury in 1961. It is pictured in Wemyss' red and ivory livery at their stance in Academy Street, Inverness at Davidson the sculptors' yard prior to departure for Fort George via Dalcross and Ardersier. Although serving a largely rural area the Wemyss Bros. business benefitted considerably from the large number of army personnel based at Fort George barracks and similarly RAF staff at Dalcross Airfield.

Although based in the neighbouring county of Morayshire, the bus routes operated by Norman Smith of Grantown on Spey lay mainly in Inverness-shire. A popular service, especially during the winter season, was that which served the Cairngorm ski grounds at Coire Cas. Duple bodied OB type Bedford SO 9111 of 1950 was purchased from Mackay's tours of Grantown and seen uplifting skiers for their return journey to Aviemore. Smith sold out in 1966 to Highland Omnibuses, but this bus was not one of those retained for further operation.

# AULTBEA - INVERNESS
# BUS SERVICE

### (SEASON 1961)
### ALTERNATE THURSDAYS ONLY FROM
### 18th MAY to 21st SEPTEMBER

| MAY | JUNE | JULY | AUGUST | SEPT. |
|------|------|------|--------|-------|
| 18th | 1st | 13th | 10th | 7th |
|  | 15th | 27th | 24th | 21st |
|  | 29th |  |  |  |

## TIME TABLE

**OUTWARD—**

| | | | | | |
|---|---|---|---|---|---|
| MELLON CHARLES | ... | ... | ... | depart | 7 0 a.m. |
| AULTBEA | ... | ... | ... | „ | 7 10 a.m. |
| POOLEWE | ... | ... | ... | „ | 7 30 a.m. |
| GAIRLOCH (Strath) | ... | ... | ... | „ | 7 50 a.m. |
| LOCH MAREE | ... | ... | ... | „ | 8 20 a.m. |
| KINLOCHEWE | ... | ... | ... | „ | 8 45 a.m. |
| INVERNESS (Farraline Bus Park) | ... | arrive | 11 20 a.m. |

**INWARD—**

| | | | | | |
|---|---|---|---|---|---|
| INVERNESS (Farraline Bus Park) | ... | depart | 6 0 p.m. |
| KINLOCHEWE | ... | ... | ... | arrive | 8 40 p.m. |
| LOCH MAREE | ... | ... | ... | „ | 9 0 p.m. |
| GAIRLOCH (Strath) | ... | ... | ... | „ | 9 30 p.m. |
| POOLEWE | ... | ... | ... | „ | 9 50 p.m. |
| AULTBEA | ... | ... | ... | „ | 10 10 p.m. |
| MELLON CHARLES | ... | ... | ... | „ | 10 20 p.m. |

## FARES

| | | | Single | Return |
|---|---|---|--------|--------|
| AULTBEA to INVERNESS | ... | ... | 14/6 | 25/- |
| POOLEWE to INVERNESS | ... | ... | 13/6 | 22/6 |
| GAIRLOCH to INVERNESS | ... | ... | 12/6 | 20/- |
| LOCH MAREE to INVERNESS | ... | ... | 10/6 | 18/- |
| KINLOCHEWE to INVERNESS | ... | ... | 9/- | 16/- |

## JOHN BAIN & SONS
### NORTH ERRADALE, GAIRLOCH
#### Phone: NORTH ERRADALE 410

Highland Printers Ltd., Inverness

J. BAIN & SONS GAIRLOCH RETURN 20/-

Apart from Highland Omnibuses, MacBraynes and Alexanders who were the big three users of Farraline Park Bus Station in the 1950s and 60s, a number of small firms arriving from country districts also shared the premises. For instance Robert Kennedy of Kilartlity journeyed in from Foxhole and Glenconvinth, and James MacIntosh came from Croy, while from the west coast MacKenzie of Garve arrived from Ullapool and John Bain of North Erradale was a fortnightly visitor on the long journey which started at Mellon Charles and served Aultbea, Poolewe, Gairloch and Kinlochewe en route to Inverness, (shared with the Achnasheen Hotel Co.). Parked at the familiar columns of Inverness library in Farraline Park is SMY 911, a classic Duple bodied Bedford OB of 1948 in silver and red livery which Bain had purchased second hand from Northern Roadways of Glasgow. Its passengers enjoyed six and a half hours in town before returning westwards. This lengthy 91 mile service proved a boon when originated in 1946 as folks from the Gairloch area had been previously unable to reach Inverness and return home on the same day. In 1964 Bain sold the service to Highland Omnibuses.

Wheels were also found on the waters of Loch Ness, Loch Oich and Loch Lochy in pre-war years. Probably the best known were those of the paddle steamer "Gondolier" which plied the waters of the Caledonian Canal from 1866 for an impressive 73 years until withdrawal in 1939 after which she was one of the vessels deliberately sunk in the waters of Scapa Flow, Orkney, to provide a blockade to enemy shipping. She was built to provide the service between Banavie on the west coast and Muirtown, Inverness, for the proprietor, David Hutcheson of Glasgow. Hutcheson was the predecessor of David MacBrayne who took over operations from 1879. Many picture post cards showed "Gondolier" negotiating the locks at Fort Augustus which gave passengers sufficient time for a spot of shopping in the enterprising local canal side stores. This early Edwardian view depicts her en route to Inverness and descending through the locks towards Loch Ness.

Nearly four decades later, "Gondolier" is again captured traversing the five locks at Fort Augustus at what was roughly the half way point on the journey. This 1938 scene shows various alterations on board the vessel which over the years had undergone several improvements to general passenger comfort and the reliability of what was by this time at 72 years of age an elderly lady. Also visible are the turrets of the now closed Benedictine Abbey on the shores of Loch Ness as "Gondolier" makes her way westwards to Banavie.

Invermoriston Pier, Loch Ness

Apart from "Gondolier" several other passenger vessels plied the Caledonian Canal, none of which, however, achieved her almost legendary status. P.S. "Lochness" for instance was built in 1853 and initially served on the Clyde as the "Lochgoil", then to Ireland as "Loch Foyle" before returning to the Clyde. David MacBrayne purchased her in 1885, renamed her once more and after a variety of structural improvements allocated her to the Caledonian Canal. This Victorian view from the early 1890s at Invermoriston pier shows her therefore when still a relative newcomer. She was scrapped in 1912. When "Gondolier" was withdrawn in 1939, regular marine passenger services ended on the Canal, although improved bus and freight services, which were also provided by MacBrayne in conjunction with MacRae & Dick, meant no suffering for the various lochside villages which lost their ferry connections.

Caravanning in Aviemore in the late 1920s when this type of vacation was gaining in popularity at a time when holidays at home were the only ones considered. Seen here with the heights of Craigellachie in the background, the Speyside resort was popular even then although few could have foreseen the major tourist developments which would take place around the village. A Buick Roadster tows a caravan, probably produced by Eccles of Birmingham, reckoned to have built Britain's first production tour caravans.